HAIRPINS
ALAIN JULES HIRWA

This is a work of fiction. All names, characters, places, and incidents are a product of the author's imagination. Any resemblance to real events or persons, living or dead, is entirely coincidental.

Published by Akashic Books
©2023 Alain Jules Hirwa
ISBN: 978-1-63614-122-0

All rights reserved
Printed in China
First printing

Akashic Books
Brooklyn, New York
Instagram, Twitter, Facebook:
@AkashicBooks
E-mail: info@akashicbooks.com
Website: www.akashicbooks.com

African Poetry Book Fund
Prairie Schooner
University of Nebraska
110 Andrews Hall
Lincoln, Nebraska 68588

TABLE OF CONTENTS

Preface by Thabile Makue 5

Lamentation 9
Restricted Colors 10
The Way of the Cross 11
Bird Migration 13
Rotten Boat 17
Museum of Curiosity 18
Hairpins 19
Hijra 20
Love Song to Cross Pollination 22
Ibereshi 24
Requiem 26

Acknowledgments 27

PREFACE
by Thabile Makue

Hairpins is a portent of eternal migration for those who leave home or are, in the words of Somali poet Warsan Shire, "spat out" by their countries. Their journey is to be long, pruning, and cavernous. The distance shall teach them, and their lantern shall be restriction.

Alain Jules Hirwa's subject matter is transition. He assesses, soberly, the ephemeral nature of countries, names, bodies, languages, and gender. If he is to steady himself, his speaker must find footing in the endless—the queer and spiritual.

We first learn of Hirwa's use of restriction as precaution in "Lamentation." "All I can claim is this, my body. I keep it like a secret." In "Restricted Colors," he takes in smoke to conceal his burning house:

> I keep my mouth shut
> for the smoke to not show off its restricted colors
> because I'm restricted to say what's inside me.

Hirwa's speaker understands that restraint is a double-edged sword—a heavy cross. He knows the lengths he is not allowed to go, the vulnerabilities he won't suffer and won't enjoy. He is tenacious in bearing this.

Hirwa provides the reader a simple formula for connecting to the work: you will glean from it whatever you are vulnerable enough to see.

And there is much to see in the opening. Beyond the meticulous form, a testament of the writer's talent and skillfulness, is an ethereal, mystical adage. The speaker's journey is like a spiritual seeker's. The more he undresses, the more he finds to peel. In this way, the loss of country is the hermit's transformative journey inward.

Hirwa's speaker traverses a haunted diaspora, with the marks of war and grief present in his connections with other migrants. They mirror his loss back to him as he reflects theirs.

> We decided to bury our mother tongues in our mouths,
> for being seen as nationals
> for being seen as insiders as real boys as normal people.
>
> We started to avoid meeting each other,
> when we'd run into each other
> you'd say Fleur
> and I'd show you a flower in my teeth and walk away.
>
> My father once told me he detests anything that reminds him of home
> of Congo
> because that thing
> that fellow migrant
> that photograph from Pointe-Noire
> will always remind him he is not home,
> which is a war
> to live in a place that sees you as an outsider, a thief, spit at your feet.
>
> ("Bird Migration")

Hirwa marks an intersection between migration and transformation, asking the reader, "Who leaves his country without the intent to change?" He makes his speaker's transition clear. At first, we see him barter with his xenophobic world, giving what he can do without and keeping much of himself hidden in caution. And then, slowly and progressively, he unfurls, exposing a new softness. His resilience grows complicated, becoming both courageous and yielding. Teaching us to recognize the bravery of reticent steps:

> Changing clothes gives a person a chance
> to different beauties.
> I choose to offer myself like a door
> that opens into another door.
> At least you get a story to tell.

("Museum of Curiosity")

The title poem, "Hairpins," is the moment of rapture—a climax of sorts. Here, we come to the nucleus of the speaker's migration story to find that it is also one of self-discovery and queerness. We see Hirwa's speaker expertly apply his knowledge of transit and in-betweenness to step beyond the gender binary. His arrival is holy. The seeker's quest is answered. He has found a real and eternal self, and he is changed.

We now encounter someone who has come into his power, whose ghosts no longer terrify, and whose vantage point is expansive, queer, and psychedelic:

> you really ran after me, and I kept running, hiding my shyness and smiles and softness
>
> you grew up running after me
> until I stopped at 23, turned, and fought back with my dreadlocks, soft weapons.
>
> So let the snakes in my skull be exposed
> and let whoever calls me a gorgon turn into stone.

("Ibereshi")

It is not presumptuous to say watch out for Alain Jules Hirwa. *Hairpins* is a stunning start. A delicate, precise, and moving promise of more to come.

LAMENTATION

Outside this room, a stranger goes by my name.
Father, I will not lie and claim to own something
that is housed far away in mouths of strangers.

All I can claim is this, my body. I keep it like a secret.

And then I will die, and the stranger will outlive me.

RESTRICTED COLORS

Tonight, he searches my face for traces
of a beauty he heard in my silence.
He wakes me up
sets my house on fire.
I close all my windows and doors
so that the smoke of the fire does not exit
but my neighbors smell the restricted
songs he sings
and violent knocks appear on the door.

He runs into his body,
and turns into my dream.

My dream transforms him into a girl
before it allows him
to pour his tears into my cup of coffee.

To wake up,
I climb the wall,
stand on the chimney,
draw in the smoke,
so that no one could know my house is on fire.

I keep my mouth shut
for the smoke to not show off its restricted colors
because I'm restricted to say what's inside me.

THE WAY OF THE CROSS

The light exists in different forms.

Sometimes
it is the freedom
that only darkness can offer.

We became alive
during nights
and died on mornings,
before we'd return
back at nights
dressed in our sisters' beads
and softness.

The dark teeth of the night chewed
our sanctuary.

Now we hide our sugar in cold drinks
or
in espresso
so that mouths do not taste our sweetness.

But no man hides stars in a night sky.
Night watchmen
smelled our perfume,

now we are afraid of daylight and its eyes,
we accompany each footstep into the day
with a rosary bead. All eyes we meet

turn into courtrooms when they see us
and each of our steps
feels like one station of the Way of the Cross.

BIRD MIGRATION

We met
on a train
to Minor Seminary,
Our Lady of Flowers,
an all-male place where the only woman
is a patron saint.

You'd later tell me
I was Our Lady of Flowers
because of my name Fleur,
French because my father was Congolese,
his presence in South Africa
a migration from a civil war.

While other such sons
of Congolese migrants
were named after wars,
my father named me after flowers.
Maybe he wanted to forget the war,
maybe he wanted to hide the war,
maybe that's why the war kept coming
back in our bloodline.
When a war is hidden
it always comes back.

On our first day at the seminary,
having not come with a parent,
you walked beside my mother as if you could be anybody's son,
something you shared with migrants,
humans ready to be citizens of any country.

When the rector asked you, *Are you with them?*
you quickly nodded
attaching yourself to strangers,
avoiding that we'd shake our heads first
cutting short a sense of belonging,
something I'd later learn you were denied by everyone,
having always been on the move
between your uncles and aunts,
always being moved into a new vase
when you were starting to fix your roots in another one's soil.
Another commonality you shared with migrants:
always on a run from places that call them migrants, thieves
spit on their feet
and chase them when they had started to make home out of hard lives.

We became each other's safe houses
the way two migrants from the same country
are each other's motherlands.
We met to remind ourselves of our mother tongues.
That's how you asked me how Zulu tasted like
Can you taste a language? I asked,
Yeah—yeah—yeah—yeah in your mouth.
I can curl my tongue in your mouth and teach myself any language
you speak.

Someone heard us speak in our mother tongue,
two migrants speaking Swahili in London,
and called us migrants, thieves, spat at our feet,

and so, they began
wars we hid inside our bodies
and so, they began
wars we hid inside our diaries.

We decided to bury our mother tongues in our mouths,
for being seen as nationals
for being seen as insiders as real boys as normal people.

We started to avoid meeting each other,
when we'd run into each other
you'd say Fleur
and I'd show you a flower in my teeth and walk away.

My father once told me he detests anything that reminds him of home
of Congo
because that thing
that fellow migrant
that photograph from Pointe-Noire
will always remind him he is not home,
which is a war
to live in a place that sees you as an outsider, a thief, spit at your feet.

Like my father, we cut the umbilical cord
before our love could birth a war,
we buried the war in the river some miles away from school
but the river is always running,
migration and running have something in common, you know?

At the end of that first year at the seminary,
my mother,

afraid that the seminary had something
that was making me queer,
changed my school to a mixed school,

but the river stretches like a serpentine being,
it reaches this new school
in a girl who swore I can drown in her.
But because the river followed me,
because a war
when hidden
will always come back,
I unburied our umbilical cord
wore it like a necklace
and dared the girl to love me

I said, *I'm bisexual
can you still love me?*

Now my classmates spit at my feet like I'm a migrant.

Father asks me to be patient
I will find you a new school next year
he says.

I take note in my head:
bird migration is a seasonal movement of queer little boys like me.

ROTTEN BOAT

to my lover / I'm a bathtub / fill me with water / lie in me and make yourself at home / I'm a stateless traveler / make me your citizen

know that the boat you're boarding / is a rotten one / that is seeking islands / to tell the stories of odds / courage and turning lemons / into lemonade

learn to hold me / as a dying man / holds his last breath / as a kid / holds water in his palms

MUSEUM OF CURIOSITY

Let's say I don't get to tell you about the boy.
Let's say I hide it.
Let's say my labyrinthine self never
shows in my soft behaviors.
Let's say I hide my plethora of selves.
Let's say I offer myself like an eternal
menu with only one single meal option.
Let's say I offer myself like an end
of curiosity.
What's the big deal?
In the end, you get bored of putting
on the same tuxedo over and over.
I mean who wouldn't?
Changing clothes gives a person a chance
to different beauties.
I choose to offer myself like a door
that opens into another door.
At least you get a story to tell.

HAIRPINS

Let's say I never mention buying hairpins at the store.
Let's say you never told me long hair was for girls.

Consider my names.
Jules is a nongendered name.
Saint is a nongendered name too.

Consider we meet on Facebook.
Consider you are the boy who texted me to ask if I am a girl.
Consider I reply that I have long hair which I tie at the back using a hairpin.

Will you conclude I am a girl with unsettled breasts and a slender body
and everything that is uninterested in revealing my gender?
Or will you say hairpins have no gender and keep asking?

HIJRA

1
This is a landlocked country
there are not enough beaches
to normalize the art of nakedness

at the campfire where we burn secrets from our mouths
I remember
Muntadhar al-Zaidi exercised freedom by opening the laces of his shoe
to mean you don't always have to open the window in your mouth in
    order to be seen,
my sign tonight is my sister plaiting my hair.

Father's free speech tonight is that bisexual boys should burn
in this campfire
à la
the starburst we roast.

2
The curse is so strong
it is able to turn my tongue into a serpent,

the snake hits my teeth &, in my father's eyes,
my teeth fall into the fire like rotten mangoes.

When I'm done
setting the names of all the boys I've loved before free from my mouth
Mother crosses herself.

3
Our Father who art in heaven
Hallowed be thy intersexuality
that merged masculinity with femininity
and
named me Hijra
the Third Gender.

4
This prayer is to explain how a moonlit night is a half-broken day
and children will watch it through windows
to pay homage to the moonlight
the mixture of daylight and night darkness
Hijra
God's magnum opus.

LOVE SONG TO CROSS POLLINATION

The body too was a landscape.
Where she touched on my body she left a religion.

Before we disemboweled our love,
I gave her a watermelon mistaking it for the lips of God,
but there was no God in it.
There was a girl and a girl making love
songs.

I covered the red shape of her kiss on my cheek with my hijab.
The translator said our kisses were planted in a wrong spot,
and where there's wrongness there's a body dancing to the song of shiver.

At the mosque, we didn't see Allah we saw a yellow zinnia
lying on the bosom of a leaf that belonged to a lavender zinnia.
Behind the mosque,
I said it reminded me of cross-pollination.

A meaning of "cross" as a noun:
an upright post with a transverse bar, as used in antiquity for crucifixion,
meaning you cross a border because you are running from crucifixion.

A meaning of "cross" as a verb:
go or extend across or to the other side of (a path, road, stretch of water,
or area), meaning you cross a border because you are looking for the
other side of something.

Where God is a border,
in a religion of colors, some people worship rainbows, they that stretch

>   beyond borders.
> One evening, she said where there is a rainbow there will be tears falling
>   from the sky.

In the religion of flowers, we underwent cross-migration.
Migrants in America, land of the free.
She's the lantern of my skull,
matchstick that lights the sun.

IBERESHI

I know you too well
and your streets know me too well too,
at 8 I feared your nights, stayed up
all night afraid that darkness would never end.
I started to keep fireflies in my pockets
you said I was being less of a man, *when will you grow up?*

At 10, I grew up, saw birds building nests in my body
inside a dream I grew up,
at 15, our national anthem no longer did justice the rush
in my blood then I grew up,
at 20, I outgrew our country's civilization.

A newspaper article carried the headline
Aspiring Rwandan writer keen to highlight issues around transgender
I started to grow up when over dinner my friend asked if I were trans.

I said, *No.*
He said, *We'd kill you.*

I grew up, being killed.
At 22, I started to run.

You filled my eyes with darkness to enable me to sleep
until my pockets started to run out of fireflies
until I started to run out of softness.

At 22, I grew up running,
you were running after me, in the girl who said, *Stop being girlie*

you were running after me, in the girl who said, *No you should cut your hair, long hair is for girls*

you really ran after me, in my new two roommates who said, *You can't play RnB in this room, only hip-hop songs are allowed on these speakers*

you really ran after me, and I kept running, hiding my shyness and smiles and softness

you grew up running after me
until I stopped at 23, turned, and fought back with my dreadlocks, soft weapons.

So let the snakes in my skull be exposed
and let whoever calls me a gorgon turn into stone.

REQUIEM
—in memory of Teddy

1
The day you fell in the battle,
you passed it down to me.

I mean, the war still lodges in my heart.

Someone once said a war never ends.
It only hides in places where it gnaws like a tick
on memories of the survivors.

It's like the dead.
They never die. They only relocate into the hearts of the living,
making the hearts heavier.

2
Changing clothes can be difficult sometimes, you know?
I'm a child refusing to take off her new dress at night
when she must put on darkness.

I'm a child refusing to leave her mother's tomb
Saying, *I'm still here with you, Ma'am.*
Before she becomes a map, her eyes two oceans
that will send out rivers that will travel memories.

ACKNOWLEDGMENTS

"Restricted Colors," and "The Way of the Cross" previously appeared as part of a lyric essay in the inaugural issue of *Lolwe*.

"Lamentation" previously appeared in *Jalada Africa*.